50 Undiscovered Ryukyu Recipes

By: Kelly Johnson

Table of Contents

- Goya Champuru
- Rafute (Okinawan Braised Pork Belly)
- Soki Soba (Okinawan Pork Rib Soba)
- Umi Budo (Sea Grapes Salad)
- Tofuyo (Fermented Tofu)
- Juushi (Okinawan Mixed Rice)
- Hirayachi (Okinawan Savory Pancake)
- Nabera no Irichi (Stir-Fried Sponge Gourd)
- Chinsuko (Okinawan Shortbread Cookies)
- Mozuku Su (Vinegared Mozuku Seaweed)
- Mimiga (Okinawan Pig Ear Salad)
- Yushi Dofu (Soft Okinawan Tofu Soup)
- Andansu (Okinawan Pork Miso Paste)
- Gurukun Karaage (Fried Banana Fish)
- Shima Rakkyo (Okinawan Shallot Pickles)
- Asa Soup (Seaweed Soup)
- Tebichi (Okinawan Simmered Pig's Feet)
- Irabu Jiru (Sea Snake Soup)
- Tachiuo no Miso Ni (Braised Beltfish in Miso)
- Nankotsu Soki (Okinawan Soft Bone Pork Rib)
- Shima Tofu Champuru (Island Tofu Stir-Fry)
- Kuba Maki (Okinawan Pork Wrapped in Kuba Leaves)
- Nigana Shiraae (Okinawan Bitter Greens with Tofu Dressing)
- Chomeiso Tempura (Longevity Herb Tempura)
- Abura Miso Onigiri (Okinawan Miso Rice Balls)
- Okinawan Purple Sweet Potato Pie
- Yambaru Chicken Soup
- Kubu Irichi (Stir-Fried Kelp)
- Okinawan Green Papaya Salad
- Okinawan Goya Tempura
- Jushi Miso Soup
- Okinawan Shikwasa Sherbet
- Mozuku Tempura
- Awamori-Marinated Sashimi
- Okinawan Brown Sugar Mochi

- Shima Udon (Okinawan Wheat Noodles)
- Beni Imo Tart (Purple Sweet Potato Tart)
- Okinawan Squid Ink Soup
- Satay Andagi (Okinawan Doughnuts)
- Goya Pickles
- Okinawan Shikwasa Juice
- Suji Soba (Okinawan Tendon Soba)
- Papaya Irichi (Stir-Fried Green Papaya)
- Okinawan Black Sugar Syrup Dessert
- Hamaguri Miso Soup (Okinawan Clam Miso Soup)
- Okinawan Red Bean Soup
- Kariyushi Rice Porridge
- Taman Yaki (Grilled Local Snapper)
- Okinawan Pineapple Vinegar Dressing
- Okinawan Shikwasa-Marinated Chicken

Goya Champuru (Okinawan Bitter Melon Stir-Fry)

Ingredients

- 1 medium goya (bitter melon)
- 200g firm tofu
- 100g pork belly (or Spam)
- 2 eggs
- 1 small onion, sliced (optional)
- 1 tbsp soy sauce
- 1 tbsp sake
- 1 tbsp mirin
- 1/2 tsp salt
- 1/4 tsp black pepper
- 1 tbsp vegetable oil
- Bonito flakes (optional, for garnish)

Instructions

1. **Prepare the Goya** – Cut the bitter melon in half lengthwise, remove the seeds, and slice into thin half-moons. Soak in salted water for 10 minutes, then drain and pat dry.
2. **Prepare the Tofu** – Wrap the tofu in paper towels, place a weight on top, and let it drain for 10–15 minutes. Cut into cubes.
3. **Cook the Tofu** – Heat oil in a pan over medium heat and fry the tofu cubes until golden. Remove and set aside.
4. **Cook the Pork** – In the same pan, cook the pork belly or Spam until slightly crispy. Add onions if using.
5. **Stir-Fry the Goya** – Add the bitter melon and stir-fry for 2–3 minutes.
6. **Combine Everything** – Return the tofu to the pan, add soy sauce, sake, mirin, salt, and pepper. Stir well.
7. **Add Eggs** – Beat the eggs and pour them over the mixture. Stir gently until just set.
8. **Serve** – Plate the dish and top with bonito flakes if desired. Enjoy warm!

Rafute (Okinawan Braised Pork Belly)

Ingredients

- 500g pork belly
- 2 tbsp awamori (or sake)
- 2 tbsp soy sauce
- 2 tbsp brown sugar
- 1 tbsp miso paste
- 1 tbsp mirin
- 1 small piece ginger, sliced
- 2 cups water

Instructions

1. Cut pork belly into large chunks and blanch in boiling water for 5 minutes. Drain and rinse.
2. In a pot, combine awamori, soy sauce, sugar, miso, mirin, and ginger. Add water.
3. Add pork and bring to a boil. Reduce heat, cover, and simmer for 2–3 hours until tender.
4. Serve with steamed rice or as a side dish.

Soki Soba (Okinawan Pork Rib Soba)

Ingredients

- 500g pork spare ribs
- 1 liter dashi broth
- 2 tbsp soy sauce
- 1 tbsp awamori (or sake)
- 1 tbsp mirin
- 1 tbsp sugar
- 1 clove garlic, minced
- 200g Okinawan soba noodles
- Green onions, sliced (for garnish)
- Red pickled ginger (beni shoga)

Instructions

1. Blanch ribs in boiling water for 5 minutes, then drain.
2. In a pot, combine dashi, soy sauce, awamori, mirin, sugar, and garlic. Add ribs and simmer for 1.5–2 hours until tender.
3. Cook soba noodles according to package instructions.
4. Serve noodles in broth, topped with ribs, green onions, and pickled ginger.

Umi Budo (Sea Grapes Salad)

Ingredients

- 100g umi budo (sea grapes)
- 1 tbsp rice vinegar
- 1 tbsp soy sauce
- 1 tsp mirin
- 1 tsp sesame oil
- 1 tsp sugar
- 1 tsp grated ginger
- 1 tbsp lemon juice

Instructions

1. Rinse umi budo gently in cold water and drain.
2. In a bowl, whisk vinegar, soy sauce, mirin, sesame oil, sugar, ginger, and lemon juice.
3. Serve umi budo with dressing on the side or lightly tossed.

Tofuyo (Fermented Tofu)

Ingredients

- 200g firm tofu
- 100ml awamori (or strong sake)
- 1 tbsp red koji mold
- 1 tbsp miso paste
- 1 tsp sugar

Instructions

1. Press tofu to remove excess water, then cut into cubes.
2. Mix awamori, koji, miso, and sugar into a paste.
3. Coat tofu cubes with the mixture and place in a sterilized jar.
4. Cover and ferment at room temperature for 2–4 weeks.
5. Serve in small portions as a delicacy with awamori.

Juushi (Okinawan Mixed Rice)

Ingredients

- 2 cups short-grain rice
- 1/2 cup pork belly, diced
- 1/2 cup carrots, julienned
- 1/4 cup shiitake mushrooms, sliced
- 1/4 cup burdock root, thinly sliced
- 1 tbsp soy sauce
- 1 tbsp mirin
- 1 tbsp awamori (or sake)
- 1 tsp salt
- 2 cups dashi broth

Instructions

1. Rinse rice and drain.
2. In a rice cooker or pot, add all ingredients and mix well.
3. Cook according to rice cooker settings or simmer covered for 15–20 minutes.
4. Let rest for 10 minutes, then fluff and serve.

Hirayachi (Okinawan Savory Pancake)

Ingredients

- 1 cup all-purpose flour
- 1/2 cup water
- 1 egg
- 1/4 tsp salt
- 1/4 cup green onions, chopped
- 1/4 cup canned tuna (optional)
- 1 tbsp sesame oil

Instructions

1. Mix flour, water, egg, and salt until smooth. Stir in green onions and tuna.
2. Heat sesame oil in a pan and pour batter in a thin layer.
3. Cook until golden brown on both sides.
4. Serve with soy sauce or ponzu.

Nabera no Irichi (Stir-Fried Sponge Gourd)

Ingredients

- 1 sponge gourd (nabera), sliced
- 100g pork belly, sliced
- 1/4 cup tofu, cubed
- 1 tbsp miso paste
- 1 tbsp soy sauce
- 1 tbsp vegetable oil

Instructions

1. Heat oil in a pan and stir-fry pork belly until browned.
2. Add sponge gourd and cook until soft.
3. Stir in tofu, miso, and soy sauce. Mix well.
4. Serve warm.

Chinsuko (Okinawan Shortbread Cookies)

Ingredients

- 1 cup cake flour
- 1/4 cup lard or butter
- 1/4 cup sugar

Instructions

1. Preheat oven to 160°C (320°F).
2. Mix flour, lard, and sugar until crumbly, then knead into a dough.
3. Shape into small logs or rounds.
4. Bake for 15–20 minutes until lightly golden.

Mozuku Su (Vinegared Mozuku Seaweed)

Ingredients

- 100g mozuku seaweed
- 2 tbsp rice vinegar
- 1 tbsp soy sauce
- 1 tsp sugar
- 1/2 tsp dashi powder

Instructions

1. Rinse mozuku and drain.
2. Mix vinegar, soy sauce, sugar, and dashi.
3. Pour over mozuku and serve chilled.

Mimiga (Okinawan Pig Ear Salad)

Ingredients

- 200g pig ears
- 1 tbsp soy sauce
- 1 tbsp rice vinegar
- 1 tsp sesame oil
- 1 tsp grated ginger
- 1 tbsp green onions, chopped

Instructions

1. Boil pig ears for 1 hour, then slice thinly.
2. Mix soy sauce, vinegar, sesame oil, and ginger.
3. Toss pig ears in dressing and top with green onions.

Yushi Dofu (Soft Okinawan Tofu Soup)

Ingredients

- 200g yushi dofu (soft tofu)
- 2 cups dashi broth
- 1 tbsp soy sauce
- 1/2 tsp salt
- Green onions, sliced (for garnish)

Instructions

1. Heat dashi broth with soy sauce and salt.
2. Add yushi dofu and heat gently.
3. Serve topped with green onions.

Andansu (Okinawan Pork Miso Paste)

Ingredients

- 200g ground pork
- 1/4 cup miso paste
- 2 tbsp sugar
- 1 tbsp awamori (or sake)
- 1 tbsp soy sauce
- 1 tbsp vegetable oil

Instructions

1. Heat oil and cook pork until browned.
2. Stir in miso, sugar, awamori, and soy sauce.
3. Simmer until thickened.
4. Store in a jar and use as a condiment.

Gurukun Karaage (Fried Banana Fish)

Ingredients

- 2 small banana fish (gurukun), cleaned
- 2 tbsp soy sauce
- 1 tbsp awamori (or sake)
- 1/2 cup potato starch
- Vegetable oil (for frying)

Instructions

1. Marinate fish in soy sauce and awamori for 30 minutes.
2. Coat in potato starch.
3. Deep-fry at 180°C (350°F) until crispy.
4. Drain and serve hot.

Shima Rakkyo (Okinawan Shallot Pickles)

Ingredients

- 200g shima rakkyo (Okinawan shallots)
- 1/2 cup rice vinegar
- 2 tbsp sugar
- 1/2 tsp salt

Instructions

1. Trim and rinse shallots.
2. Boil for 30 seconds, then cool.
3. Mix vinegar, sugar, and salt.
4. Pour over shallots and let sit for 3 days before eating.

Asa Soup (Seaweed Soup)

Ingredients

- 10g dried asa seaweed
- 2 cups dashi broth
- 1 tbsp soy sauce
- 1/2 tsp salt
- 1/2 tsp miso paste (optional)

Instructions

1. Rehydrate seaweed in water for 5 minutes, then drain.
2. Heat dashi with soy sauce and salt.
3. Add seaweed and simmer for 2 minutes.
4. Serve hot.

Tebichi (Okinawan Simmered Pig's Feet)

Ingredients

- 2 pig's feet, cleaned and halved
- 1 piece ginger, sliced
- 2 tbsp awamori (or sake)
- 2 tbsp soy sauce
- 1 tbsp miso paste
- 1 tbsp sugar
- 1 liter dashi broth
- 2 green onions, chopped (for garnish)

Instructions

1. Boil pig's feet for 10 minutes, then drain and rinse.
2. In a pot, combine dashi, ginger, awamori, soy sauce, miso, and sugar.
3. Add pig's feet and simmer for 2–3 hours until tender.
4. Serve with chopped green onions.

Irabu Jiru (Sea Snake Soup)

Ingredients

- 1 dried sea snake (irabu), soaked overnight
- 1 liter dashi broth
- 1 piece kombu (kelp)
- 1 tbsp awamori (or sake)
- 1 tbsp soy sauce
- 1/2 tsp salt

Instructions

1. Cut soaked sea snake into pieces.
2. In a pot, bring dashi, kombu, and awamori to a boil.
3. Add sea snake and simmer for 2 hours.
4. Season with soy sauce and salt before serving.

Tachiuo no Miso Ni (Braised Beltfish in Miso)

Ingredients

- 2 beltfish fillets
- 2 tbsp miso paste
- 1 tbsp soy sauce
- 1 tbsp mirin
- 1 tbsp sugar
- 1 cup dashi broth
- 1 small piece ginger, grated

Instructions

1. In a pot, mix dashi, miso, soy sauce, mirin, sugar, and ginger.
2. Bring to a simmer and add beltfish fillets.
3. Cover and cook for 10–15 minutes.
4. Serve warm with rice.

Nankotsu Soki (Okinawan Soft Bone Pork Rib)

Ingredients

- 500g pork ribs (soft bone)
- 1 liter dashi broth
- 2 tbsp soy sauce
- 1 tbsp awamori (or sake)
- 1 tbsp mirin
- 1 tbsp sugar
- 1 piece ginger, sliced

Instructions

1. Blanch ribs in boiling water for 5 minutes, then drain.
2. In a pot, combine dashi, soy sauce, awamori, mirin, sugar, and ginger.
3. Add ribs and simmer for 2 hours until soft.
4. Serve hot.

Shima Tofu Champuru (Island Tofu Stir-Fry)

Ingredients

- 200g shima tofu (firm Okinawan tofu)
- 100g pork belly, sliced
- 1/2 cup bean sprouts
- 1/2 cup cabbage, shredded
- 1 tbsp soy sauce
- 1 tbsp awamori (or sake)
- 1 tbsp vegetable oil

Instructions

1. Heat oil in a pan and fry pork belly until browned.
2. Add tofu and cook until lightly golden.
3. Stir in cabbage, bean sprouts, soy sauce, and awamori.
4. Stir-fry until vegetables are tender, then serve.

Kuba Maki (Okinawan Pork Wrapped in Kuba Leaves)

Ingredients

- 200g pork belly, sliced
- 4 kuba (screw pine) leaves
- 1 tbsp soy sauce
- 1 tbsp awamori (or sake)
- 1 tbsp mirin

Instructions

1. Marinate pork in soy sauce, awamori, and mirin for 30 minutes.
2. Wrap pork slices in kuba leaves and secure with toothpicks.
3. Steam for 30 minutes until tender.
4. Serve warm.

Nigana Shiraae (Okinawan Bitter Greens with Tofu Dressing)

Ingredients

- 100g nigana (Okinawan bitter greens)
- 100g firm tofu
- 1 tbsp miso paste
- 1 tbsp sesame seeds
- 1 tsp sugar

Instructions

1. Blanch nigana in boiling water for 30 seconds, then drain.
2. Mash tofu with miso, sesame seeds, and sugar to form a dressing.
3. Toss nigana with tofu dressing and serve.

Chomeiso Tempura (Longevity Herb Tempura)

Ingredients

- 100g chomeiso (longevity herb)
- 1/2 cup tempura flour
- 1/2 cup cold water
- 1 egg yolk
- Vegetable oil (for frying)

Instructions

1. Mix tempura flour, cold water, and egg yolk to make a light batter.
2. Heat oil to 170°C (340°F).
3. Dip chomeiso in batter and fry until crispy.
4. Drain and serve with tempura sauce.

Abura Miso Onigiri (Okinawan Miso Rice Balls)

Ingredients

- 2 cups cooked rice
- 2 tbsp andansu (Okinawan pork miso)
- 1 sheet nori (seaweed), cut into strips
- 1/2 tsp sesame seeds

Instructions

1. Wet hands and shape rice into small balls.
2. Stuff with andansu and reshape into onigiri.
3. Wrap with nori and sprinkle with sesame seeds.
4. Serve warm or at room temperature.

Okinawan Purple Sweet Potato Pie

Ingredients

- 2 Okinawan purple sweet potatoes, boiled and mashed
- 1/2 cup condensed milk
- 1/4 cup sugar
- 1 egg yolk
- 1 pre-made pie crust

Instructions

1. Preheat oven to 180°C (350°F).
2. Mix mashed sweet potatoes with condensed milk, sugar, and egg yolk.
3. Pour filling into the pie crust.
4. Bake for 25–30 minutes until set.
5. Let cool before serving.

Yambaru Chicken Soup

Ingredients

- 200g Yambaru chicken (or free-range chicken), chopped
- 4 cups dashi broth
- 1 tbsp soy sauce
- 1 tbsp awamori (or sake)
- 1/2 tsp salt
- 1/2 cup daikon radish, sliced
- 1/2 cup carrots, sliced
- 2 green onions, chopped (for garnish)

Instructions

1. In a pot, bring dashi broth to a boil.
2. Add chicken, daikon, and carrots, then simmer for 30 minutes.
3. Stir in soy sauce, awamori, and salt.
4. Serve hot, garnished with green onions.

Kubu Irichi (Stir-Fried Kelp)

Ingredients

- 50g dried kombu (kelp), soaked and sliced
- 100g pork belly, sliced
- 1/2 carrot, julienned
- 1 tbsp soy sauce
- 1 tbsp mirin
- 1 tbsp vegetable oil

Instructions

1. Heat oil in a pan and fry pork belly until browned.
2. Add kelp and carrots, stir-frying for 3 minutes.
3. Stir in soy sauce and mirin, cooking until well mixed.
4. Serve warm.

Okinawan Green Papaya Salad

Ingredients

- 1 small green papaya, shredded
- 100g pork belly, sliced
- 1 tbsp soy sauce
- 1 tbsp rice vinegar
- 1 tsp sugar
- 1/2 tsp salt
- 1 tbsp sesame oil

Instructions

1. Blanch papaya in boiling water for 1 minute, then drain.
2. Heat sesame oil in a pan, fry pork belly until crispy.
3. Mix soy sauce, vinegar, sugar, and salt.
4. Toss papaya and pork belly with dressing before serving.

Okinawan Goya Tempura

Ingredients

- 1 goya (bitter melon), sliced
- 1/2 cup tempura flour
- 1/2 cup cold water
- 1 egg yolk
- Vegetable oil (for frying)

Instructions

1. Mix tempura flour, water, and egg yolk.
2. Heat oil to 170°C (340°F).
3. Dip goya slices in batter and fry until golden.
4. Drain and serve with tempura dipping sauce.

Jushi Miso Soup

Ingredients

- 2 cups cooked juushi (Okinawan mixed rice)
- 2 cups dashi broth
- 1 tbsp miso paste
- 1/2 cup tofu, cubed
- 1/4 cup green onions, sliced

Instructions

1. Bring dashi to a boil and dissolve miso paste.
2. Add tofu and simmer for 3 minutes.
3. Stir in juushi rice and heat through.
4. Serve with green onions.

Okinawan Shikwasa Sherbet

Ingredients

- 1 cup shikwasa juice
- 1/2 cup sugar
- 1 cup water
- 1/2 cup condensed milk

Instructions

1. Heat water and sugar until dissolved, then cool.
2. Mix with shikwasa juice and condensed milk.
3. Freeze, stirring every 30 minutes until smooth.
4. Serve chilled.

Mozuku Tempura

Ingredients

- 100g mozuku seaweed
- 1/2 cup tempura flour
- 1/2 cup cold water
- 1 egg yolk
- Vegetable oil (for frying)

Instructions

1. Mix tempura flour, water, and egg yolk.
2. Heat oil to 170°C (340°F).
3. Dip mozuku in batter and fry until crispy.
4. Drain and serve with tempura sauce.

Awamori-Marinated Sashimi

Ingredients

- 200g fresh fish (tuna, snapper, or amberjack), sliced
- 1 tbsp awamori
- 1 tbsp soy sauce
- 1 tsp mirin
- 1/2 tsp grated ginger

Instructions

1. Mix awamori, soy sauce, mirin, and ginger.
2. Marinate fish slices for 5 minutes.
3. Serve chilled with wasabi and shiso leaves.

Okinawan Brown Sugar Mochi

Ingredients

- 1 cup glutinous rice flour
- 1/2 cup water
- 1/4 cup Okinawan brown sugar
- 1/4 cup kinako (roasted soybean flour)

Instructions

1. Mix rice flour and water into a smooth dough.
2. Steam for 10 minutes until sticky.
3. Knead in brown sugar until dissolved.
4. Coat with kinako before serving.

Shima Udon (Okinawan Wheat Noodles)

Ingredients

- 200g Okinawan udon noodles
- 4 cups dashi broth
- 100g pork belly, sliced
- 1 tbsp soy sauce
- 1 tbsp awamori
- 1/2 tsp salt
- Green onions, sliced

Instructions

1. Boil noodles and drain.
2. In a pot, bring dashi to a simmer, adding pork, soy sauce, awamori, and salt.
3. Cook until pork is tender.
4. Serve noodles in broth, topped with green onions.

Beni Imo Tart (Purple Sweet Potato Tart)

Ingredients

- 2 Okinawan purple sweet potatoes, boiled and mashed
- 1/2 cup condensed milk
- 1/4 cup sugar
- 1 egg yolk
- 1/2 tsp vanilla extract
- 1 pre-made tart crust

Instructions

1. Preheat oven to 180°C (350°F).
2. Mix mashed sweet potatoes with condensed milk, sugar, egg yolk, and vanilla.
3. Spoon filling into the tart crust.
4. Bake for 20–25 minutes until set.
5. Let cool before serving.

Okinawan Squid Ink Soup

Ingredients

- 1 squid, cleaned and sliced
- 2 cups dashi broth
- 1 tbsp squid ink
- 1 tbsp soy sauce
- 1 tbsp awamori (or sake)
- 1/2 tsp salt
- 1/2 cup tofu, cubed

Instructions

1. Heat dashi broth in a pot and bring to a simmer.
2. Add squid, soy sauce, awamori, and salt.
3. Stir in squid ink and tofu, then cook for 5 minutes.
4. Serve hot.

Satay Andagi (Okinawan Doughnuts)

Ingredients

- 1 cup all-purpose flour
- 1/2 cup sugar
- 1 tsp baking powder
- 1 egg
- 2 tbsp milk
- 1/2 tsp vanilla extract
- Vegetable oil (for frying)

Instructions

1. Mix flour, sugar, and baking powder in a bowl.
2. In another bowl, whisk egg, milk, and vanilla.
3. Combine wet and dry ingredients into a dough.
4. Roll into small balls and deep-fry at 170°C (340°F) until golden.
5. Drain and serve warm.

Goya Pickles

Ingredients

- 1 goya (bitter melon), thinly sliced
- 1/2 cup rice vinegar
- 1 tbsp sugar
- 1/2 tsp salt

Instructions

1. Soak sliced goya in salted water for 10 minutes, then drain.
2. Mix vinegar, sugar, and salt in a bowl.
3. Add goya and marinate for at least 1 hour before serving.

Okinawan Shikwasa Juice

Ingredients

- 1 cup shikwasa juice
- 2 tbsp honey or sugar
- 2 cups cold water
- Ice cubes

Instructions

1. Mix shikwasa juice with honey or sugar until dissolved.
2. Add cold water and stir well.
3. Serve over ice.

Suji Soba (Okinawan Tendon Soba)

Ingredients

- 200g Okinawan soba noodles
- 100g beef tendons, boiled until soft
- 4 cups dashi broth
- 1 tbsp soy sauce
- 1 tbsp awamori
- 1/2 tsp salt
- Green onions, sliced

Instructions

1. Cook soba noodles and drain.
2. In a pot, simmer dashi with soy sauce, awamori, and salt.
3. Add beef tendons and simmer for 10 minutes.
4. Serve noodles in broth, topped with beef and green onions.

Papaya Irichi (Stir-Fried Green Papaya)

Ingredients

- 1 small green papaya, shredded
- 100g pork belly, sliced
- 1/2 carrot, julienned
- 1 tbsp soy sauce
- 1 tbsp mirin
- 1 tbsp vegetable oil

Instructions

1. Heat oil in a pan and fry pork belly until browned.
2. Add papaya and carrot, stir-frying for 3 minutes.
3. Stir in soy sauce and mirin, cooking until well combined.
4. Serve warm.

Okinawan Black Sugar Syrup Dessert

Ingredients

- 1/2 cup Okinawan black sugar (kokuto), chopped
- 1/4 cup water
- 1 tsp cornstarch (optional, for thickening)
- 1 tbsp water (for cornstarch slurry)

Instructions

1. In a saucepan, combine black sugar and water over low heat, stirring until dissolved.
2. Simmer until slightly thickened.
3. If needed, mix cornstarch with water and stir into the syrup to thicken.
4. Drizzle over mochi, ice cream, or pancakes.

Hamaguri Miso Soup (Okinawan Clam Miso Soup)

Ingredients

- 6 hamaguri (clams), cleaned
- 3 cups dashi broth
- 1 tbsp miso paste
- 1 tbsp sake
- 1/2 tsp soy sauce
- 1/4 cup green onions, sliced

Instructions

1. Heat dashi broth in a pot and bring to a simmer.
2. Add clams and cook until they open.
3. Dissolve miso paste in a small bowl with broth, then stir it into the pot.
4. Add sake and soy sauce, then serve with green onions.

Okinawan Red Bean Soup

Ingredients

- 1/2 cup azuki beans, soaked overnight
- 3 cups water
- 1/4 cup Okinawan black sugar (kokuto)
- 1/2 tsp salt
- 1/2 cup mochi or sweet rice dumplings (optional)

Instructions

1. Drain soaked beans and boil in fresh water until soft (about 1 hour).
2. Add sugar and salt, then simmer until thickened.
3. Serve warm with mochi or rice dumplings.

Kariyushi Rice Porridge

Ingredients

- 1/2 cup cooked rice
- 2 cups dashi broth
- 1/2 tsp salt
- 1 tbsp soy sauce
- 1 egg, beaten
- 1/4 cup green onions, chopped

Instructions

1. Bring dashi broth to a simmer and add rice.
2. Stir in salt and soy sauce, cooking until soft.
3. Slowly drizzle in beaten egg while stirring.
4. Serve hot, garnished with green onions.

Taman Yaki (Grilled Local Snapper)

Ingredients

- 1 whole taman (local snapper), cleaned
- 1 tbsp soy sauce
- 1 tbsp awamori (or sake)
- 1 tbsp mirin
- 1/2 tsp salt
- 1 tbsp vegetable oil

Instructions

1. Rub snapper with salt and let sit for 10 minutes.
2. Mix soy sauce, awamori, and mirin, then brush over the fish.
3. Heat oil in a grill pan and cook fish for 4–5 minutes per side until crispy.
4. Serve warm with a side of pickled vegetables.

Okinawan Pineapple Vinegar Dressing

Ingredients

- 1/4 cup pineapple juice
- 2 tbsp rice vinegar
- 1 tbsp honey
- 1 tbsp olive oil
- 1/2 tsp salt
- 1/4 tsp black pepper

Instructions

1. Whisk all ingredients together in a bowl.
2. Drizzle over salads, grilled meats, or seafood.
3. Store in the fridge for up to a week.

Okinawan Shikwasa-Marinated Chicken

Ingredients

- 2 chicken thighs
- 1/4 cup shikwasa juice
- 1 tbsp soy sauce
- 1 tbsp awamori (or sake)
- 1 tbsp honey
- 1/2 tsp salt
- 1 tbsp vegetable oil

Instructions

1. Mix shikwasa juice, soy sauce, awamori, honey, and salt in a bowl.
2. Marinate chicken for at least 1 hour.
3. Heat oil in a pan and cook chicken until golden and cooked through.
4. Serve with rice or salad.

www.ingramcontent.com/pod-product-compliance
Lightning Source LLC
LaVergne TN
LVHW081506060526
838201LV00056BA/2969